W9-CUT-838

BEYOND

BEYOND

BEYOND

BEYOND

BEYOND

THE STAFF OF LIFE »«‹ Kief Adler

THE STAFF OF LIFE »«‹ Kief Adler

THE STAFF OF LIFE »«‹ Kief Adler

THE STAFF OF LIFE »«‹ Kief Adler

THE STAFF OF LIFE »«‹ Kief Adler

NATUREGRAPH

Library of Congress Cataloging in Publication Data CIP

Adler, Kief, 1951–
    Beyond the staff of life.

    Includes index.
    1. Vegetarian cookery.   I. Title.
TX837.A3   641.5'636   76-43076

Copyright © 1976 by Kief Adler

1990 Printing.

ISBN   0-87961-076-X Cloth Edition
ISBN   0-87961-075-1 Paper Edition

Books for a better world

Naturegraph Publishers, Inc., Happy Camp, California 96039

For Warren Raysor, whose elimination of wheat and dairy products started the wheels turning, and for David Schwammel who taught me how to eat, among other things.

Also a million thanks to all those not mentioned here (you know who you are).

CONTENTS

INTRODUCTION

In the past fifteen years, we have seen a tidal wave of natural-food cookbooks spilling over the shelves of bookstores throughout the country. Each one, it seems, offers the paradisaic life to those individuals who would switch to whole grains and make the transition to the wholesome foods of yesteryear. Times change, however, and the growing, harvesting and packaging methods of the past have given way to the machine age. New evidence is emerging to alter certain premises of the natural foods diet until now it is apparent that many of these foods, specifically wheat (grains), dairy products and salt, may not be the strong, body-building foods we once thought they were. In fact, this new evidence has indicated quite the contrary.

DAIRY PRODUCTS

To begin a discussion about dairy products, we must go back to the one common source: the cow. The cow that roamed the pastures in Christ's time would certainly be unrecognizable today. Two thousand years ago the average cow produced about two hundred to two hundred and fifty pounds of milk a *year*. Today, after two thousand years of selective breeding, hormonal injections and forced feeding, modern science has turned our once contented "Bossy" into a veritable milk machine that can now produce in excess of ten thousand pounds of milk annually!

For the cow, this overproduction is causing an increase in diseases (including leukemia—a disease they never had in the past). Couple this with the artificial insemination practices which began thirty years ago and you now have a cow that lives a 20% shorter life than it did as few as fifty years ago!

But what does all this mean to the consumer of dairy products? On the one hand, this increased production yields a thinned-out product lacking in vitamins and minerals and containing an improper hormonal balance. On the other hand, milk (dairy products) has been linked to arthritis, heart disease, and dental cavities. Further, it is estimated that up to one-half the world's population is allergic, in some way, to dairy products. These allergies can cause such disorders as "eczema, recurrent ear infections, nasal congestion, abdominal bloating, irritability, asthma, fatigue, joint pains, and others."[1]

Some of the more shocking evidence of the harmful effects of milk appeared in the *Southern Medical Journal* of May 1975. Dr. Calvin W. Woodruff has shown through his experiments that the protein in milk can inflict minor injuries in the intestinal tract, with resultant hidden bleeding and a continuous loss of iron-laden red blood cells. Although the exact mechanism for this process is, as yet, unknown, this loss of iron results in the condition of iron deficiency anemia. To the teenage consumer, who has been known to drink quarts of milk a day, this is a serious problem. However, Dr. Woodruff offers two solutions to this problem. In his research he has found that gently simmering the milk for about ten minutes modifies these proteins and renders them harmless. Naturally, this heating process destroys most of the vitamins in the milk, so supplements are advised. Soy milk is also an acceptable substitute here, though the taste is, admittedly, quite different.

Dr. Woodruff recommends that mothers nurse their infants. Breast milk, although containing less iron than cow's milk, does not contain these harmful proteins, and research has again shown that the baby stores the iron it receives as a fetus and uses this iron throughout its first two years of growth. "For mothers of young children, the message is clear. Nurse your baby and you'll have no problem with damaging proteins!"[1]

J. I. Rodale, perhaps the most outspoken proponent of natural foods, comes to these conclusions concerning dairy products:

"Scientific evidence from reliable sources all over the world has shown milk and milk products to be less than the jewels of good health we were formerly led to believe they are."[2]

1. "Milk, the Imperfect Food," *Prevention* (Emmaus, PA: Rodale Press, Inc., November 1975).
2. J. I. Rodale, editor. *The Complete Book of Food and Nutrition.* (Emmaus, PA: Rodale Press, Inc., 1966).

Beatrice Trum Hunter, author of *Consumer Beware* and *The Natural Foods Cookbook*, states that "the Eskimos, the Maori, the Australian Aboriginals and other groups of people whose traditional diets did not include dairy products, nevertheless maintained themselves in good health".[3] Further, it should be noted that these primitive peoples were all free of dental cavities until they came into contact with civilization—its dairy products, as well as other highly refined foods.

In regarding this question of the use or nonuse of dairy products, it is most important to remember that all mammals, except certain groups of humans, discontinue the use of milk as a food after weaning.

SALT

Salt, that great preserver of foods, is far from being a preserver of life. It has been shown to increase the susceptibility to, if not cause, circulatory diseases. It is a principal factor in kidney trouble and heart disease. Because of its habit-forming qualities, salt (sodium chloride) has been defined as a drug by the U.S. Food and Drug Administration.

Salt is a stimulant—and a harsh one at that. Its over-stimulation of body and nerve cells can cause premature aging when taken in great excess. However, any type of stimulation causes the body to overwork itself. In the book, *Chemistry of Food and Nutrition*, Dr. Henry C. Sherman states that "through over-stimulation of the digestive tract, salt may interfere with the absorption and utilization of the food."[4] This is particularly true of calcium, whose absorption level in the body decreases as the intake of salt increases.

Drs. Robert Belliveau and Elizabeth Marsh illustrated through their research (*Archives of Pathology*, May 1961) that sodium chloride (common salt) had a detrimental effect, exacerbating atherosclerosis (hardening of the arteries) and myocardial and renal infarctions (loss of blood supply caused by circulatory obstruction in heart muscle and kidney).

Research by Dr. G. Douglas Talbott (*Annals of Internal Medicine*,

3. Beatrice Trum Hunter. *Consumer Beware!* (New York: Simon and Schuster, 1971).
4. J. I. Rodale, editor. *The Complete Book of Food and Nutrition*. (Emmaus, PA: Rodale Press, Inc., 1966).

February 1961), comparing the natural-food diet of primitive man and the processed-food diet of modern man, indicates that the further man's diet is removed from natural foods, the greater his craving for salt becomes. This helps explain man's great use of salt today. Dr. Talbott also notes that occurrences of heart disease follow this same ratio: incidence of heart disease has increased with the use of salt.

Still other research has found that sodium chloride causes a significant increase in the blood content of triglycerides, which are strongly suspected of being the most active (lipid) factors in hardening of the arteries (atherosclerosis).

It should be noted here that research has found no significant differences between table salt and sea salt, except that the latter contains an abundance of trace minerals and natural iodine. Kelp, however, is a natural seaweed product (available in powdered form) that is one of the richest sources of minerals and the best source of trace minerals. From a nutritional standpoint, it is an excellent substitute for salt.

Obviously, a certain amount of salt in our bodies is essential, but this quantity of sodium chloride is readily available in most natural foods. As J. I. Rodale states in *The Health Seeker*, "The body does need some salt to operate, but this need is adequately filled by that which is contained in natural foods. When the body gets more than is necessary, trouble begins".[5]

WHEAT

"This whole thing about the importance of bread as the staff of life leaves me cold. I think the average person is better off to entirely restrict the use of bread".[6]

"I am definitely against any wheat or rye product for human consumption . . . . What is the best program for a person who wishes to live to 120? I say don't eat bread. It is the worst form of starch. . . . It is not an edible starch".[7]

5. J. I. Rodale. *The Health Seeker.* (Emmaus, PA: Rodale Press, Inc., 1962).
6. J. I. Rodale, editor. *The Complete Book of Food and Nutrition.* (Emmaus, PA: Rodale Press, Inc., 1966).
7. Ibid.

These are but a few of the comments J. I. Rodale has to make about wheat and wheat products, and he is but one of the many nutritionists who speak out against this type of food. One should be aware that the bread spoken of here refers to *all* breads: those found on the supermarket shelf, and those made at home from 100% organic whole wheat.

What is wrong with wheat? First, it is an extremely fattening food. One reducing method currently used by doctors consists of merely removing wheat and rye products from the diet—with a guaranteed loss of some twenty pounds in two months! Bread and grains are the most common contributory causes of colds, a fact proven by medical research in which families were asked to eliminate bread and grains from their diet for one year. The results: few to no colds that year and the absence of most allergy symptoms among those who formerly suffered from them.

Among other research, Dr. Alvarez (of the Mayo Clinic) has verified that bread can pass through the whole of the small intestine without being digested at all! He further asserts that wheat interferes with the absorption of other foods, in much the same way as salt does.

Grains fill people up, giving them a false feeling of hunger satisfaction. As a result they eat less of fruits and vegetables and develop vitamin deficiencies.

"Wheat is the greatest culprit among foods in connection with the causing of allergic effects," states Dr. Albert H. Rowe, world renowned expert in the field of bronchial asthma, and a leader in allergy research.[8] In tests on some five hundred allergy sufferers, Dr. Rowe found wheat to be the cause of over one-third of their allergies. Wheat is particularly detrimental in the treatment of eczema, hives and migraines.

OTHER GRAINS

Sir Edward Mellanby, a noted British nutritionist, in his recent investigation of cereal grains (specifically oats), found a substance in these

8. Ibid.

grains that robs the body of calcium. This substance is called phytate or phytic acid and is found in especially large quantities in oats and, consequently, oatmeal. A diet high in cereals, especially oatmeal, would induce a condition of rickets, according to his findings.

Fortunately for us, there are two grains which spare us these afflictions: rice and millet. The inhabitants of the wet regions of South Asia subsist on rice, soybeans, sweet potatoes, some vegetables, bamboo sprouts and large quantities of leafy greens—no milk or milk products, and no wheat. These people are better developed physically, have more capacity for work and endurance, escape skeletal defects in childhood, and have perfectly sound, healthy teeth. Similar claims can be made for the natives of Africa who use millet, sesame seeds and cayenne pepper. Ann Wigmore, the founder-director of Hippocrates Health Institute of Boston, calls millet the queen of grains, as it is unique in being the only grain that is a complete protein (that is, contains all eight essential amino acids in their proper balance). Millet is also the only alkaline grain (whereas rice is relatively neutral, while wheat and rye are acid-forming).

Nuts and seeds are excellent substitutes for grains. Most are very high in protein and equally high in minerals, especially trace minerals and phosphorus. Although nuts are normally not great sources of vitamins; peanuts, in their raw state with skins intact, contain great amounts of B vitamins (especially thiamin) and have more pantothenic acid, by weight, than any other food except liver. They are also a good source of Vitamin E.

Sesame seeds also are a source of complete protein, and supply more calcium than any other food: 1160 mg. per 100 grams. This represents about ten times the amount of calcium in an equal amount of cows milk! Rich in vitamin E and a good source of lecithin, sesame seeds were the first seed crop to be cultivated by man.

Seeds contain a wealth of iron, phosphorus, magnesium, and B vitamins. Sunflower and pumpkin seeds are also rich in zinc, necessary for the health of the prostate gland. There is evidence that seeds enhance intelligence, and much research is being done in this area. Seeds then, like nuts, are another important class of foods to include in your diet.

CONCLUSIONS

The evidence presented in these few pages represents only a small part of the vast amount of research conducted on the dietary effects of salt, wheat, and dairy products. However, the evidence should be clear: for a healthful life, stay away from those foods—and this book can show you how! Through selection of balanced and complementary protein sources you can learn to replace these outworn traditional foods with delicious new foods of superior nutritional quality.

The ultimate choice, of course, is yours. Like any other part of your life, your diet is a personal thing. Only you can decide what is right for you and what you feel most comfortable doing. You might want to try an experiment by eliminating the salt, wheat and dairy foods from your diet for a few months, judging the results for yourself. In any event, whether you choose to follow these guidelines or not, the following recipes will certainly add a new dimension to your culinary capabilities.

Kief

Windsor, California
January, 1976

BEFORE YOU REACH FOR THE POTS AND PANS . . .

Complete proteins are an essential part of any diet. I have tried, wherever possible, to create complete proteins in these recipes.

The following food combinations will effect a complete protein:

Grains and Legumes   Seeds and Legumes

This represents a general formula only, and one should note that rice and sesame, corn and soy also supply excellent proteins that are exceptions to the general rule.

All measurements given are standardized as follows:

1 C = one 8-ounce *measuring* cup, scraped level
1 T = one *measuring* tablespoon, scraped level
1 t = one *measuring* teaspoon, scraped level

Always set *electric* ovens 25° *lower* than the temperatures given.

An asterisk (*) after a listed ingredient in a recipe indicates that this ingredient can be *made* from a recipe found in this book.

Mixing implies using a large (wooden) spoon; *beating* indicates the use of an electric mixer or egg beater (if unavailable, mix vigorously by hand).

When a recipe calls for oil, I recommend only olive or sesame oil be used. Use olive oil in recipes wherein the oil is not directly heated, and sesame when sautéeing is called for.

There are two salt substitutes that are used in these recipes. One is a mineral salt derived from ocean and land plants, the other is kelp, a natural seaweed product extremely high in minerals and trace minerals. There are also various soy sauce substitutes on the market. Your natural-food store should stock these as well as all other ingredients listed herein. If you do not care to use a salt substitute, however, simply eliminate the use of salt in the recipes. This will not affect the consistency of the product.

Ground beans (legumes) make excellent flours. However, the moisture content of the beans will vary from crop to crop; hence some of these recipes will list *approximate* amounts for liquid ingredients, as the exact quantity will vary according to the dryness of the beans.

Baking powder should always be considered an *optional* ingredient. I have included its use in some of these recipes only for those who wish to use it. Each recipe will come out perfectly without it, though the consistency will naturally be somewhat heavier. If you do use baking powder, I recommend that a low-sodium, non-aluminum product be employed.

Honey should be raw, unfiltered, and unheated, just as it comes from the comb.

I cannot recommend too strongly the use of organic fruits, vegetables, flours, etc., if available, for their purity and healthful qualities as well as their delicious flavor.

I would also urge you to use (glazed) cast iron or stainless steel for top-of-stove cookware, and glass or ovenware for baking, as these materials will not affect the taste of your food.

Finally, please take your time while cooking food. A meal created during a hectic rush will taste like it. Always remember that love is the underlying ingredient in any recipe. Each recipe in this book has been carefully tested and is 100% reliable. They have been created in response to a basic need for good, sound nutrition. Use them, share them, and help to pass on a good thing.

BEGINNING WITH BREAKFAST

INSTANT BREAKFAST
For those on the run. . .

1 C dried fruit   1 C water

Blend until smooth.

SUNFLOWER ORANGE BLEND
A recipe from the subtropics. Grab a spoon and dig in.

2 oranges, peeled and chopped   3 T sunflower seeds

1/2 C diced pineapple

Blend until very smooth.

TODAY'S DATE
A variation on an old theme sure to produce some pleasant surprises.

6 large baking apples   1/4 C cashew pieces

3/4 C soft dates, pitted and chopped   Maple syrup and cinnamon

Core apples and peel off some of their skin on one end. Combine dates and cashew pieces. Arrange apples in baking dish, fill with date mixture, drizzle maple syrup on top and sprinkle with cinnamon. Bake at 350° ½ hour or until soft.

APPLICIOUS
Take a step beyond the fruited salad.

2 large apples, grated	1/3 C alfalfa sprouts
1/3 C sunflower seeds	1 T honey
1/4 C raisins	Juice of 1 lemon

Combine apples, raisins and seeds. Mix honey and lemon juice. Arrange sprouts on top of apple mixture, pour honey and lemon juice over all and serve.

PLUTONIAN CEREAL

Try this one with your favorite fruit juice or nut milk, or serve it plain. You can also try adding enough honey to create a paste and use this as a spread on breads and muffins.

1/2 C sunflower seeds	1/4 C almonds
1/4 C pumpkin seeds	2 T carob powder (optional)
1/4 C sesame seeds	

Place all ingredients in blender and mix until well ground.

NUTS N' NANAS

A tasty way to beat the "oh no, oatmeal again!" syndrome.

2 T each of: sunflower seeds,	2 large apples, grated
sesame seeds, pumpkin seeds,	1/2 C raisins
almonds, brazil nuts	2 bananas, sliced
1/4 C shredded coconut	

Grind the nuts and seeds in a blender. Combine with remaining ingredients.

DAVID'S SESAME BANANA

Eat it with a spoon or dip your favorite bread. A calcium rush.

1/2 C sesame seeds	Water
1 large or 2 small bananas	

Grind seeds 1-2 minutes in blender. Add banana, broken in pieces, and enough water to blend.

You can vary this recipe by using other seeds, nuts or combinations.

DESERT PUDDING

A bowl full of sand dunes. Add raisins, coconut, sesame seeds, cinnamon, substitute soaked dried fruit for the banana or whatever. Don't forget to make seconds.

For each serving:

Soak 1/3 C millet in 1 C water overnight. Pour into blender along with 1 large or 2 small bananas and blend until smooth. Pour into saucepan and cook over low heat, stirring frequently, until the mixture thickens.

SIMPLE RICE OR MILLET

The best way to cook these cereals is to soak them for at least 8 hours before cooking them. This starts the sprouting process going, which increases the vitamin content. Try cooking the soaked grain in a covered pot in the oven at 150° for a few hours. If you forget to turn on the oven, here's the traditional way:

For 1 C of rice or millet

Boil 2 C water for rice, 2½ C for millet, and add the grain a little at a time so that the water never stops boiling. Boil rapidly for 2 minutes, then cover and turn heat down as far as it will go. Cook rice about 45 minutes, millet for 30.

THE BIG APPLE
You might not need honey in this cereal if the raisins you use are very sweet. Serves 4.

1 C millet	1 C chopped dried apples
3 C water	1 t cinnamon
1 C raisins	

Soak the millet in the water overnight. Bring to a boil and cook slowly until almost done, about 20 minutes. Add fruit and cinnamon and cook until done, about 10 more minutes.

BAKED SESAME RICE
Like having rice pudding for breakfast. Serves 4.

2 C cooked brown rice	1 1/2 C sesame milk*
1 C raisins	Honey

Combine rice, raisins and sesame milk adding honey to taste. Pour into deep casserole dish, cover and bake for 45 minutes at 325° F.

GOING BANANAS WITH CORN BREAD
Idea from the Doc, recipe by Kief. A winner!

1 large or 2 small bananas, sliced	2 t baking powder
1/2 C raisins	1 C corn meal
1 apple, diced	1 C soy flour
1/2 C almonds, chopped	3 T honey
1 t cinnamon	1 1/2 C water

Toss first 5 ingredients in a bowl and set aside. Pour 2 T oil in a 10" cast-iron skillet and heat in oven for 5 minutes. Combine corn meal, soy flour and baking powder, and set aside. Mix honey and water and add to flour mixture, stirring well. Spread fruit on bottom of skillet. Pour batter over all. Bake at 400° F for 20 minutes until brown on edge.

BANANA RICECAKES
You just can't miss with these. First prize every time.

1/3 C cashews	1 T honey
1 1/4 C warm water	1 T dry active yeast
3/4 C rice flour	2 T oil
1/4 C soy flour	1/4 t nutmeg
1/4 t mineral salt	1 large or 2 small bananas

Combine all ingredients, except bananas, in blender, blending until smooth. Let rise 45 minutes to 1 hour. Add the bananas in mashed or *chopped* form (mashed bananas have a tendency to stick when cooked). Cook on lightly oiled griddle until brown; turn and cook other side.

ALL AROUND PANCAKES

Try adding raisins or chopped fruit and don't spare the maple syrup. This recipe also makes excellent crepes if you thin the batter by adding more water. Take care to avoid tearing the crepes as these will be more fragile than their wheated counterparts. The crepes are delicious when filled with sautéed vegetables or stewed fruits.

1/3 C soy flour	Pinch mineral salt
1/3 C lima bean flour	1 T oil
1/3 C corn meal	3/4 C water
2 T honey	2 t baking powder

Combine ingredients by hand or in a blender. Cook on well oiled griddle until brown, then turn and cook other side.

BASIC CORNCAKES

The corn meal gives a naturally sweet taste to these pancakes. Add sesame seeds for a nutty flavor.

1/2 C soy flour	1 T honey
1/2 C corn meal	1 T oil
3/4 C water	

Combine ingredients by hand or in a blender. Cook over medium flame on an oiled griddle.

APPLE CORNCAKES

Use whatever variety of apples you prefer and serve with applesauce-in-the-raw* for a special breakfast.

1 C corn meal	1 T honey

1/4 C soy flour	2 1/2 T oil
1/2 t mineral salt	1 C apple juice or water
1 t cinnamon	1 C grated apple

Combine all ingredients in a large bowl, stirring well. Cook on well oiled griddle as in preceding recipes.

BLUEBERRY SOYCAKES
Stock up when the blueberry season starts—you'll want these every day. Tasty.

1 C soy flour	2 T honey
1/3 C lima bean flour	2 T oil
1 C water	1 C blueberries

Blend first 5 ingredients until smooth. Fold in blueberries. Cook on oiled griddle as in preceding pancake recipes.

DRINKS AND DRAUGHTS

NUT OR SEED MILK
This is the basic recipe used throughout this book. Smaller quantities can be made by using the same proportions of nuts or seeds to water.

1 C nuts or seeds   4 C water

Mix in blender on highest speed 2-3 minutes. Strain if desired.

FRESH COCONUT MILK
You owe it to yourself to try this version.

1 fresh coconut   Hot water

Break open the coconut, pouring the clear milk into the blender. Chop the coconut meat and place in blender. Add enough hot water to bring the level to 4½ C. Blend at high speed for 3 minutes, strain, wringing pulp, then return pulp to blender, just cover with hot water and blend again at high speed for 2 minutes. Strain, wring out pulp and discard.

SOY MILK
Make as you need, so it is fresh.

2-3 T soy milk powder   2 C water

Liquefy soy milk powder and water in blender.

SUNRISE
>Wake up to this one.

1 apple, chopped   Juice of 6 carrots

1 orange, chopped

>Liquefy in blender.

DAVID'S TIBETAN THIRD EYE TONIC
>For the cyclops in all of us.

2 C orange juice   1 papaya, diced

>Blend

ISLAND HOP
>Take a trip to the South Seas without leaving your kitchen.

1/4 C pineapple juice   3/4 C carrot juice

Juice of 2 oranges

>Blend.

BLUE MOON
>"Now I'm no longer alone. . ."

1 C blueberries   1/4 C soy protein powder

1 C apple juice   1/4 C or more water

>Blend, adding more water, if desired, for a thinner juice.

NO. 9, MU-APPLE LANE
A great thirst quencher for those hot summer days.

1 part apple juice   Fresh mint leaves

1 part Mu tea no. 9

Blend juice with cool tea. Add mint leaves to taste and blend again.

STRAWBERRY-BANANA SMOOTHIE
When you're not making them into preserves, try using your strawberries this way.

1 banana   1/2 C strawberries

1/2 C apple juice   2 ice cubes

Blend well until ice disintegrates.

APRICOT COOLER
Nectar for the Gods.

1 1/2 C apricot juice   2 C vanilla ice cream*

1 C nut or seed milk*

Blend.

ALMOND APPLE MILK
When it's apple time, it's time for this one.

1/2 C ground almonds   2 C apple juice

2 T brewers yeast

Blend well.

OPEN SESAME
Magic in a glass.

1/4 C sesame seeds   1 C water

1 banana

Blend well.

CAROB-BANANA SHAKE
You can use nut milk instead of water for a richer, thicker shake.

1 1/4 C water   1 large or 2 small bananas

2 T carob powder   2 T soy protein powder

Honey to taste

Blend.

HOT HOLIDAY CIDER
After you've warmed their hearts, this one will take care of their bodies.

4 C apple cider   2 C black cherry juice

Juice of 6 oranges   Cinnamon sticks

1/4 C lemon juice

Combine in saucepan and heat on stove. Serve with cinnamon sticks.

MERRY CHRISTMAS
. . . and a Happy New Year, too. Says it all.

4 C apple juice

2 C pineapple juice

2 C orange juice

1 C cranberry or cherry juice

Juice of 3 lemons

2 oranges, sliced

1/2 t nutmeg

Mix juices in a large bowl, drop in the orange slices and sprinkle with the nutmeg.

CARROT MILK
Affectionately known as the "orange cow".

1/2 C carrot juice

1/2 C soy milk*

1/4 C sesame seeds

Blend well.

VEGETABLE COCKTAIL
A body builder.

1 beet

3 carrots

1 tomato

1 small yellow squash

2 stalks celery

Few sprigs parsley

Kelp and black pepper

Juice vegetables and add seasonings to taste.

TOMATO JUICE PLUS
Put some zip in your tomatoes.

4 medium tomatoes, chopped

2 green onions, chopped

1 T chopped parsley

Pinch marjoram

1/8 t black pepper

1 t kelp

Blend well.

KIDNEY KLEANSER
A tonic from the past to help your kidneys.

1 part cucumbers

1 part carrots

1 part beets

Juice.

LIME TIME
Another summertime favorite.

Juice of 6 limes

4 C water

Honey to taste

Blend.

SOUPS

VEGETABLE STOCK

Save the soak water from sprouting beans and seeds, the water left after you steam vegetables, all your vegetable scraps (ends of carrots, tips of vegetables, etc.) plus a few fresh vegetables, a small handful of assorted herbs and water to cover all. Simmer gently for about 2 hours, strain and use in making any soup or by itself as a hot vegetable drink.

LIFE RAFTS ON THE SEA OF GREEN
The soup that never lets you drown.

2 onions, chopped	1 large carrot, sliced
3 T oil	2 large Jerusalem artichokes,
1 T oregano	sliced
1 T basil	Mineral salt and black pepper
1/2 T thyme	2 T soy sauce substitute
2 C green split peas	1 C cooked brown rice
7 C water	

Sauté onions in the oil until tender. Add the herbs and split peas and continue sautéeing for 1 more minute. Add the water, carrot and artichoke, bring to a boil and simmer gently about 1 ½ hours until the split peas are tender. Stir in rice and seasonings and cook for 10 more minutes.

QUASAR SOUP
The soup that takes you away. . .

1 onion, chopped	1 T oregano
3 T oil	Mineral salt and black pepper

2 ribs celery, chopped

1 1/2 C black beans

6 C stock

1 t celery seed

Juice of 1/2 lemon

Sauté onion, oregano and celery seed in oil for 5 minutes. Add celery and cook another 2 minutes. Add beans and stock, bring to a boil and simmer for 2-3 hours until the beans are soft. Add lemon juice and seasonings and serve.

GINNY'S POTATO SOUP
A recipe from the soup queen of Mandala Cafe.

3 large potatoes, chopped and
   steamed

1 large onion, diced

2 T oil

Mineral salt and black pepper

6 C sesame milk*

1 T turmeric

1 T dill

1 T basil

Heat the sesame milk in a large pot with the turmeric, dill, mineral salt and pepper. Mash the potatoes, leaving small lumps, and add to milk mixture. Sauté the onions in the oil until clear, add to potato mixture and simmer for 30 minutes to 1 hour.

MAGIC MUSHROOM SOUP
Something worth hunting for. . .

1 lb mushrooms, sliced

3 T oil

1 t thyme

1 t marjoram

4 C sesame milk*

1 bunch green onions, chopped

1 3/4 C water

1/4 C soy sauce substitute

Sauté the mushrooms and herbs in a large saucepan for 5 minutes in the oil. Add the green onions and cook until the mushrooms are just soft. Add the milk and water and bring to a boil. Simmer gently for 1 hour, add soy sauce substitute and serve.

MICHAEL'S MINESTRONE
Just like the old country.

1/4 C oil	2 C dry garbanzo beans, cooked
3 onions, diced	10 C tomato purée
3 celery hearts, diced	1 T each oregano, basil,
3 carrots, diced small	marjoram
2 C sliced mushrooms	Pinch of cayenne and cumin
1/3 head cabbage, shredded	Mineral salt

Sauté herbs and onion in oil until clear. Add vegetables, except cabbage, and sauté until barely soft. Add tomato purée, beans, cabbage and seasonings. Simmer for 1 hour until vegetables are cooked.

MYSTICAL ONION SOUP
The secret of a good onion soup is to sauté the onions very slowly until they are well browned. Try it, you'll like it.

3 large onions	1 T tarragon
6 C well seasoned stock	1/4 C oil

Chop the onions in half and cut in very thin slices. Sauté over a low flame for 20-30 minutes until well browned. Meanwhile heat the stock and tarragon. When the onions are done, add to stock and simmer for 1 hour.

SPECTRUM SOUP

Bright orange and green on a creamy white background. Smooth and delicious.

2 large bell peppers, halved and sliced	4 C stock
	2 C soy milk*
2 large carrots, sliced	1 t thyme
2 onions, halved and sliced	1 t oregano
3 T oil	Mineral salt and black pepper

Sauté the herbs and onion in the oil until clear. Add vegetables and cook 1 minute. Add stock and soy milk and simmer for 1 hour. Season and serve.

JACK FLASH ASPARAGUS SOUP

The fastest soup I know.

2 C soy milk*	1 t thyme
2 C cashew milk*	1 t mineral salt
2 C asparagus pieces	White pepper

Combine all ingredients in blender. Bring to a boil and simmer slowly for 1/2 hour.

NOVEMBER'S MYSTERY SOUP

Conceived in Scorpio and dedicated to a higher consciousness. A meal in itself.

1 yellow onion, chopped	10 C water
1 red onion, chopped	3/4 C small white beans
1/4 C oil	1 C chopped spinach or chard

1 T oregano	Mineral salt, cayenne, black
1 T basil	pepper, cumin
3 C carrot chunks	Juice of 1 lemon
2 C yellow split peas	

Sauté onion, basil and oregano in oil in a large pot until just golden. Add carrots and cook another 5 minutes. Add split peas and mix to coat with oil. Add water and bring to a boil. Add white beans, spinach or chard and seasonings, and simmer for 2 hours until beans are cooked. Add lemon juice, adjust seasonings and serve.

CREAM OF CARROT SOUP
The carrots give this soup its naturally sweet taste and beautiful orange color.

10 carrots	1 C water
3 T oil	Mineral salt and black pepper
7 C stock	2 t thyme
1 T arrowroot	1/4 C chopped parsley
1/2 C soy milk powder	

Chop carrots into small pieces and sauté with the thyme for 5 minutes. Add the stock and cook until carrots are soft. Add seasonings, liquefy in blender and return to heat. Blend water, arrowroot and soy milk powder and add to soup while stirring constantly. Simmer gently for 30 minutes, add parsley and serve.

SPINACH AND LENTIL SOUP
A Turkish soup with an infinite number of variations. This is the basic recipe.

1 C green or brown lentils	1 tomato, chopped
1 lb fresh leaf spinach, chopped	1/8 t cayenne
1 large onion, chopped	Mineral salt
3 T oil	6 C water or stock

Cook the lentils in the water or stock for 1 to 1-½ hours, until soft. Sauté the onion in the oil until golden brown. Add the spinach and sauté over low heat, covered, about 5 minutes. Add onions and spinach to the lentils with the tomato, mineral salt and cayenne. Simmer for 30-60 minutes and serve.

RED LEB LENTIL SOUP
The soup that always makes the right connections.

3 T oil	2 C red lentils
2 onions, chopped	8 C stock
4 cloves garlic, pressed	1 T cumin
1 celery heart, chopped	4 bay leaves
1 carrot, chopped	Mineral salt and black pepper

Sauté the onion and garlic in the oil until golden. Add stock, lentils, celery, carrot and bay leaves and cook for 1 hour. Add seasonings and simmer an additional 15 minutes.

SALADS AND DRESSINGS

SPROUTING

There is no better way of eating seeds, grains and legumes than by sprouting them first. The nutritional changes that occur are staggering: starch is converted to simple sugars, the vitamin C level increases up to 500%, the B-vitamin complex increases by as much as 1000% and the protein is directly converted into amino acids, making any sprout virtually a predigested food. Your growing sprouts, exposed to some light, will also produce chlorophyl. Even the soak water that begins the sprouting process becomes a rich source of water-soluble vitamins and minerals.

There are several sprouting containers available commercially that are quite adequate, yet I prefer to use a wide-mouth quart canning jar covered by either a piece of wire screening cut to fit the lid or a piece of cheesecloth secured by a rubber band.

Wash the seed first, then place in your jar with twice as much water as seed. Leave in a dark place (like a cabinet), pour off (and save) the soak water and rinse the seeds 2-3 times daily. Leave them in the sunlight for their last 24 hours, to produce chlorophyl. The following instructions will help you to sprout the seeds of your choice. Always remember to store your sprouts in the refrigerator.

SMALL SEEDS (such as alfalfa, radish, chia, and fenugreek)

Soak 2 T of seed in ½ to 1 C water for 6 hours. Drain. Rinse 3 times daily. Leave in darkness for 3 days, then light for 3 days. Sprouts are best when about 1-½ to 2 inches in length.

MEDIUM SEEDS (such as lentil, mung and soy beans)

Soak 1 C seeds in 2 C water for 16 hours. Drain, rinse

twice daily for about 3 days. Leave in light for last 24 hours. Lentils are best when 1", mung about 1-½" and soybeans about ½" long.

LARGE SEEDS (such as garbanzo or any large bean)

Soak 1 C seed in 2-3 C water for 24 hours. Drain and sprout for 3-5 days until sprouts are ½"-¾" long.

WHOLE EARTH SPROUT SALAD
A delicious way to discover sprouts.

1 C alfalfa sprouts	1/2 avocado, chunked
1 carrot, shredded	1/4 C red onion, chopped
1/2 green pepper, sliced	Mandala Herb Dressing*

Toss in a large bowl, add dressing and toss again.

SPROUT SLAW
Any eggless mayonnaise can be used in the dressing.

1/2 C lentil sprouts	1 clove garlic, pressed
1/2 C mung sprouts	1 T kelp
1 C red cabbage, shredded	1/2 t mustard powder
1 carrot, grated	1/4 t ginger, pinch of cayenne
2 T soyonaise*	

Toss vegetables and sprouts. Combine remaining ingredients, pour over vegetables, toss and serve.

MANDALA SALAD
From the menu of the restaurant by the same name.

1 C red leaf lettuce, chopped

1 C romaine lettuce, chopped

1/4 C celery pieces

1/4 green pepper, sliced

Few slices cucumber

1/2 tomato cut in 4 wedges

1 green onion, chopped

1/4 C red cabbage, chopped

1/4 C shredded carrot

1/4 avocado, sliced

Toss lettuce, celery, cucumber, green onion, cabbage and carrot. Arrange tomato, green pepper and avocado slices on top, dress with any dressing, top with alfalfa sprouts, sprinkle with sesame seeds, and serve.

MY SALAD
Developed under David's watchful eyes.

4 large leaves red leaf lettuce

1 carrot, shredded

1 medium beet, shredded

1/2 avocado, chopped

1/2 tomato, chopped

Juice of 1/2 lemon

1 C sprouts

1 T kelp

2 (or more) cloves garlic,

    pressed

1 T olive oil

2 T soyonaise*

Tear lettuce into pieces. Add carrot, beet, avocado and tomato and toss. Add kelp, garlic, lemon juice, olive oil, and soyonaise and mix well. Add sprouts and serve.

PYRAMID SALAD
This salad is so beautiful to look at you might use it as a centerpiece at your next party.

3 C finely chopped romaine lettuce

2 tomatoes, sliced

1 large carrot, grated

1 red onion, diced

1 large cucumber, sliced	3 T chopped parsley
1 large beet, grated	Mid-East Dressing*

Arrange lettuce on bottom of a large round plate. Cover all but the outer 1-½" of the lettuce with tomato slices. Repeat this procedure with the cucumber, followed by the beet, then the carrot and topped by the onion, always making each circle 1-½ to 2 inches smaller then the preceding one. Sprinkle with parsley and drizzle dressing over all.

POTATO SALAD WITH A TWIST
For the cocktail hour. . .

4 C steamed, sliced potatoes	3 T lemon juice
3 T chopped parsley	1 t mustard powder
1 bell pepper, diced	1/2 t black pepper
1 bunch green onions, chopped	1 t mineral salt
2/3 C soyonaise*	

Gently mix the cooled potato slices with the parsley, bell pepper and green onions. In another bowl, combine the remaining ingredients, pour over the potatoes and toss well.

HERB ROAD COLE SLAW
A recipe developed on a warm spring morning in May.

1 green cabbage, cored and shredded	4 cloves garlic, pressed
	3-4 T lemon juice
4 large carrots, grated	2 T kelp
2/3 C soyonaise*	1 T honey

1/4 C olive oil   1 T poppy seeds

Mix cabbage and carrots well. Make the dressing by combining the remaining ingredients. Pour over the vegetables and mix very well. NOTE: Any cole slaw will taste superb after it has marinated for 24 hours, so plan to make this one a day ahead of time.

SWEET POTATO SALAD
Try it for breakfast.

4 sweet potatoes, baked and   2 diced apples

   cut in cubes   1 C raisins

4 small bananas, sliced   1/2 t nutmeg

Mix together well and serve.

SUMMERTIME FRUIT SALAD
A beautiful way to greet the summer sun.

1 banana, sliced   1/2 C seedless grapes

1/4 pineapple, cut in chunks   Juice of 1 lemon

1/2 papaya, cut in chunks   Juice of 1 orange

1 peach, cut in chunks   2 T shredded coconut

Chop the fruit into a bowl, sprinkle with the lemon and orange juice and top with coconut.

WHERE'S RAINER'S BIG BANANA SALAD
A tribute to a 2-year-old wonderchild.

2 big bananas, sliced   1/4 C raisins

1/4 lb dried peaches, soaked overnight	1/4 C chopped walnuts

Chop the peaches and toss with the bananas and raisins. Sprinkle with walnuts and serve.

APPLE SALAD
A refreshing salad for snacks or any time.

4 apples, grated	1/4-1/2 t nutmeg
3/4 C currants	1/4 t cinnamon
1/2 lb ground walnuts	

Combine ingredients and serve.

APPLESAUCE-IN-THE-RAW
If you've never tasted raw applesauce, you're in for a treat.

2 apples, chopped	1/2 t cinnamon
Juice of 1/2 lemon	1/4 t allspice
1/4 C raisins	Water

Place apples, spices and lemon juice in blender. Liquefy, adding just enough water to allow ingredients to blend. Stir in raisins and add honey, if desired.

GUACAMOLE
It seems that no cookbook could be complete without this recipe—and for good reasons, too.

2 ripe avocados	1/8-1/4 t cayenne

2 cloves garlic, pressed	1 t cumin
1 t kelp	1/2 onion, minced
Juice of 1 lime	1/2 tomato, diced

Mash the avocados with a fork. Add garlic, kelp, cayenne and cumin and mix well. Fold in remaining ingredients.

HUMMUS
Perhaps the most popular of all middle eastern foods.

1 C dry garbanzo beans	1 t paprika
Juice of 2-3 lemons	1 carrot, grated
3 cloves garlic, pressed	1 T olive oil
1/2 C sesame butter	Mineral salt
1 T parsley	

Soak the garbanzos overnight in 3 C water. Drain and cook until soft, 2-3 hours. Mash or grind the beans (or purée them in a blender) until they make a soft paste. Add the remaining ingredients and mix very well. Serve on bread or with vegetable dippers.

SOYONAISE
A rich, creamy mayonnaise-type dressing that can be used in so many recipes. It's the olive oil that gives this dressing its superior taste.

1 C water	3 T lemon juice
1/2 C soy milk powder	2 T apple cider vinegar
1/2 t mineral salt	1 t dill
1 C olive oil	

In blender liquefy the soy milk powder and the water. Slowly add the oil with blender at its highest speed. Pour into a bowl. Add the mineral salt and dill and mix with a wire whip. Now add the vinegar and lemon juice while you continue to whip the dressing. Store in refrigerator.

THE CANDYMAN'S NIRVANA SALAD DRESSING

The candyman and I are now 3000 miles apart. Before he left California he gave me this recipe—one of the best salad dressings I know.

1 C chopped carrots	1 t mineral salt
1 C chopped parsley	2 t dill
1/4 lb tofu (soy cheese)	2 cloves garlic, pressed
2/3 C olive oil	1/4 C soysauce substitute
1/2 C sesame butter	Water

Liquefy the ingredients in batches in a blender, adding water to facilitate blending when necessary. Thin dressing with water to desired consistency.

MID-EAST DRESSING

The most popular salad dressing in the Middle East.

3/4 C olive oil	1/2 t black pepper
1/4 C lemon juice	2 cloves garlic, pressed
1/2 t mineral salt	

Shake well in a jar.

MANDALA HERB DRESSING
A flavorful wheel of herbal tastes.

2 t each: marjoram, dill, basil,	Pinch of cayenne
oregano and thyme	1 C apple cider vinegar
2 cloves garlic, pressed	3 C oil

Combine in a bottle and shake well.

ROSEMARY'S 1000 ISLAND DRESSING
A gift from a flower to a garden.

1 large potato, baked	1/2 t thyme
Olive oil	3 T chopped onion
1 tomato	3 T chopped pickle
1 t basil	1 t mustard powder
1 t oregano	cayenne

After the potato has cooled, mash it with enough olive oil to make a thick paste. Put tomato and herbs through blender. Mix with potato. Add onion, pickle, mustard and cayenne (to taste) and thin with water as needed. Mix well.

BIG RED
. . . Able to dress an entire salad in a single glob!

1/4 C + 2 T olive oil	1 t oregano
2 T lemon juice	1/2 t thyme
4 C chopped tomatoes	2 T sesame butter
2 t kelp	1/4 t black pepper
1 t basil	

Liquefy in blender.

AVOCADO DRESSING
Sometimes I wonder how people can live without these lovely green fruits.

1 avocado, chunked	Pinch of cayenne
2 chopped green onions	1 t kelp
1 clove garlic, pressed	Water
Juice of 1 lemon	

Place ingredients in blender with enough water to just blend.

FRENCH DRESSING
The old stand-by.

1 C olive oil	1 t kelp
1 C tomato juice, pieces or sauce	1 T paprika
1 C lemon juice or apple cider vinegar	2 T honey

Combine in a jar and shake very well.

SUNSHINE DRESSING (for fruit salads)
The proper attire for any fruit salad.

1 C pineapple chunks	Orange juice
1 golden delicious apple	

Blend apple and pineapple with enough orange juice to liquefy.

VEGETABLES, GRAVIES AND SAUCES

TOFU

This is the Oriental soybean curd or cheese that one finds in most Chinese grocery stores. Its uses are limited only by your own imagination. Here are three different methods for its preparation.

FROM DRY SOYBEANS

Soak 1 C soybeans in 4 C water overnight. Drain off liquid and wash beans very well. Liquefy in blender—adding 1 C water to each ½ C beans—for 3 minutes. Strain through a fine sieve, saving both the water and the pulp. Return pulp to blender and just cover with water. Liquefy this mixture for 2 minutes and strain into rest of liquid. Discard pulp.

Bring liquid to a boil in the top of a double boiler, stirring constantly. Add the juice of 2 lemons, stirring just enough to mix juice into liquid. Allow mixture to stand in heat (without stirring) until it coagulates. Remove from heat immediately and cool.

FROM SOY MILK

Pour 1 quart of soy milk* into a bowl and leave in a warm place until it sours and thickens. When thick, cut into large chunks with a knife. Place these chunks in a saucepan, cover with water and bring to a boil. Pour into a sieve lined with cheesecloth and wring curds as dry as possible.

FROM SOY FLOUR

Mix 1 C soy flour with enough cold water to make a paste. Beat for 1 minute with a mixer and add to 3 C boiling water. Simmer for 5 minutes, add the juice of 2 lemons and remove from heat. When cool, strain through cheesecloth or a fine sieve.

ASPARAGUS BAKE
A recipe discovered during the dawning of the age of asparagus in spring.

1 lb asparagus	1/4 C sunflower seeds
1/2 C corn meal	Cayenne and mineral salt
1/4 C rice flour	1 C tomato sauce*

Hold the asparagus spear by its ends, and snap it. Save the tip end and discard the remainder of the spear. Mix the corn meal, rice flour, sunflower seeds, mineral salt and cayenne. Oil a 9 x 5 loaf pan. Arrange a layer of ½ of the asparagus followed by ½ the corn meal mixture and ½ of the tomato sauce. Repeat with the remaining ingredients and bake at 350° for 30-45 minutes until asparagus is tender.

BASIL IN THE LIMAS
A simple and savory side dish sure to enhance any meal.

1 C dry lima beans	Mineral salt and black pepper
1 T oil	1 T basil
1 onion, diced	

Bring the limas to a boil with 3 C water. Boil 5 minutes, cover and let stand off heat for 1 hour. Add oil, onion, basil and seasonings and cook 45-60 minutes until beans are soft. Add water as needed while cooking.

EGYPTIAN CAULIFLOWER
From the land of the Pharaohs . . .

1 cauliflower	Juice of 1 lemon
1 T oil	

Break cauliflower into flowerets and steam for 2 minutes. Heat oil in skillet and add cauliflower. Sauté until barely tender, sprinkle with lemon juice and let sit, covered, on a very low flame until tender.

CURRIED CAULIFLOWER AND EGGPLANT
A passage to India. . .

1 cauliflower, separated into	2 t mineral salt
flowerets	2 cloves garlic, pressed
1 medium eggplant, cut in 1" cubes	1/8-1/4 t cayenne
1/4 C oil	1/4 t each coriander and cumin
1 t black mustard seeds	Juice of 1 lemon
1/2 t turmeric	1 tomato, cut in wedges

Heat the oil, add the mustard seeds and cook until they pop. Add cauliflower and turmeric, and sauté for 3 minutes. Add ½ C water, cover and cook on LOW for 5 minutes. Add eggplant, garlic and spices and cook, uncovered, for 3 minutes. Add about 1 C water and cook, covered, for 15 minutes on MEDIUM until tender. Add tomato and lemon juice, mix and serve.

BAKED EGGPLANT SLICES
A great snack, too!

1 eggplant	Thyme and oregano
Oil	Kelp

Slice eggplant into ½" rounds, brush with oil and arrange on baking sheet. Sprinkle with thyme, oregano and kelp, and bake for 10 minutes at 350°, then turn the slices and bake another 5-10 minutes until tender.

GREEN BEANS WITH SUNFLOWER SEEDS
A variation of green beans almondine.

1 lb green beans	White pepper
1 T oil	1/2 C sunflower seeds
Water	1 1/2 t basil
Juice of 1 lemon	

Cut ends off beans, and slice diagonally into 1" sections. Heat the oil, add the green beans and basil, and sauté for 2 minutes. Add a few tablespoons of water, cover and steam on LOW for 5 minutes. Add lemon juice, white pepper and sunflower seeds, cover and steam for 3 minutes until tender.

MUSHROOMS, PEPPERS AND ONIONS
Just add rice for a tasty fried-rice main dish.

1/2 lb mushrooms, sliced	2 t basil
1 large bell pepper, chopped	1 t thyme
1 large onion, chopped	Pinch of cayenne
3 T oil	Mineral salt

Sauté the onion in the oil for 2 minutes, then add the pepper, mushrooms, basil and thyme and continue to sauté for another 5 minutes. Add mineral salt and cayenne, cover and cook over low flame for an additional 2 minutes.

SOUTHERN BLACK-EYED PEAS
A terrific dinner when complemented with cornbread and a green salad.

2 C dry black-eyed peas	6 C water

2 large tomatoes, chopped

1 large onion, diced

1 T paprika

1/4 t cayenne

3 cloves garlic, pressed

1 T cumin

2 T oil

Combine the peas and water and boil for 5 minutes. Cover and let sit for 1 hour. Add tomato, onion, paprika, cayenne, garlic, cumin and oil, and simmer covered for 2 hours, stirring occasionally.

UNIDENTIFIED FLYING POTATOES
You'll be glad when these land in your oven.

2 lbs potatoes

1/2 t black pepper

2 T oil

1/2 C chopped chives

1 t mineral salt

Paprika

Slice the potatoes and steam them until soft. Add the oil, mineral salt and pepper, and mash well. Stir in chives. Form into 2" balls and place on an oiled baking sheet, flattening the bottom only. Sprinkle with paprika and bake for 30 minutes at 350° until brown.

SPICED WINTER SQUASH
A pie without the crust . . .

1 small acorn or butternut
   squash

Pinch of cloves

Pinch of allspice

1 T oil

1/4 t cinnamon

1 T honey

1/4 t mineral salt

Cut the squash in half and remove the seeds. Combine

the remaining ingredients in a small bowl and brush this mixture on the squash halves. Arrange in baking dish and bake for 45-60 minutes at 350° until soft.

MUSHROOM CLOUD GRAVY
Watch out for the leeks.

2 C sliced mushrooms	1 t thyme
1 leek, chopped	2 C coconut milk*
2 T oil	2 T soy sauce substitute
1 t oregano	1 T arrowroot

In a saucepan, sauté the leeks and mushrooms in the oil with oregano and thyme for 5 minutes. Mix arrowroot with coconut milk and soy sauce substitute. Add to saucepan and simmer until thick, stirring frequently.

THE CHAIRMAN'S GRAVY
A traditional Chinese gravy that goes well with any sautéed vegetable dish.

1 T arrowroot	1/2 t ginger
2 C stock*	1 t soy sauce substitute
White pepper	

Mix the arrowroot with the stock in a saucepan. Add remaining ingredients and simmer until thickened, stirring frequently.

NICE TOMATO SAUCE
The friendly red one . . .

24 ripe tomatoes, chopped	1 T oregano
1 large bell pepper, diced	1/2 T thyme
1 large onion, diced	1/4 t cayenne
1/4 C chopped parsley	2 t mineral salt
4 cloves garlic, pressed	1/2 t black pepper
2 T basil	1/4 C olive oil

Sauté the onions, bell pepper, garlic and herbs in the oil until the onion just starts to turn golden. Add remaining ingredients, cover and simmer for several hours. Stir occasionally and reseason if necessary.

SESAME SAUCE
A "cream salad" from the Sahara.

2 cloves garlic, pressed	1 t cumin
1/2 C lemon juice	3 T chopped parsley
1/2 C sesame butter	Mineral salt and white pepper

Combine all ingredients in blender and season to taste.

ALMOND SAUCE
A deliciously rich sauce for rice or vegetables.

2/3 C almonds	1 clove garlic, pressed
2 C water	1/2 t honey
1/2 t mineral salt	1/4 t turmeric
1/4 t white pepper	Juice of 1 lemon

Combine all ingredients and blend well. Simmer for 20-30 minutes until thick, stirring frequently.

GINGER YAM SAUCE
More, more . . .

3 yams

2-3 t grated fresh ginger

Pinch of white pepper

Pinch of mineral salt

Water

Bake yams until very soft, peel, mash well. Add ginger, mineral salt and pepper, mixing well. Add water to thin to desired consistency and simmer for 5-10 minutes until hot.

MASOOR DAL
A lentil sauce from India.

1 C red lentils

4 C water

1 t mineral salt

1/4 t each cumin, ginger, tur-meric, cayenne, and coriander

Juice of 1/2 lemon

Boil the lentils in water for 5 minutes, then lower heat, cover and cook for 30 minutes or until lentils are soft. Stir in spices and mineral salt and simmer for 15 minutes. Add lemon juice and serve.

GARLIC CHUTNEY
Take a voyage to the center of the sun.

10 cloves garlic, pressed

1 t cayenne

1 t coriander

1/2 t cumin

1 t honey

Mash ingredients together with a fork.

MAIN DISHES

THE NO PIZZA PIZZA

It may not look like the real thing, but the taste goes it one better.

1/2 C soy flour	3/4 C tomato sauce*
1/2 C corn meal	1 bell pepper, sliced
1 T oil	1 onion, diced
1 T honey	1 C sliced mushrooms
1/2 t mineral salt	1/2 lb tofu, sliced*
1/2 C water	

Mix the soy flour, corn meal and mineral salt, then add the oil, honey and water. Spread mixture about ¼" thick on an oiled baking sheet, making a ridge around the edge to hold the sauce. Spread tomato sauce on crust, followed by the onion, peppers and mushrooms. Cover with thin slices of tofu. Bake at 325° until crust is done and vegetables are tender, about 30 minutes.

SPACE BALLS

Strange visitors from another planet disguised as tofu croquettes.

2 C tofu*	2 C cooked brown rice
1 T oil	1/4 C chopped parsley
1/2 t kelp	1/4 T each oregano, thyme, sage
1/2 C chopped chives	Corn meal

Mix all ingredients, except corn meal, vigorously by hand. Form into small balls (or flat cakes), roll in corn meal and bake on an oiled baking sheet 30 minutes at 350°. Serve with your favorite sauce or gravy.

BEANS N THINGS
Tortillas or chapatis complement this dish perfectly.

1 C white beans	1 onion, chopped
1 C cauliflower pieces	1/2 C chopped celery
1 C broccoli pieces	1 T kelp
2 C chopped tomato	1 t paprika
1 T molasses	1/4 t thyme
1/2 t cayenne	1 1/2 t basil

Cook the beans in about 3 C water for 2 hours until tender. Place beans in a large mixing bowl, add remaining ingredients and mix very well. Pour into a deep casserole dish, cover and bake for 1 hour at 350°.

LENTIL AND VEGETABLE STEW
For those new to lentils, this dish is sure to open your eyes.

1 C lentils	1 onion, chopped
2 potatoes, chunked	2 T oil
2 medium zucchini, sliced	2 cloves garlic, pressed
2 carrots, sliced	2 T chopped parsley
2 stalks celery, sliced	Juice of 2 lemons
Mineral salt and black pepper	

Cook the lentils in 2-½ C water for 1 hour until almost soft. Add the potatoes, zucchini, carrots, celery and mineral salt and pepper to taste. Cook for 20 minutes, adding water as needed. Sauté the onion and garlic in the oil until golden. Add to lentils with the lemon juice and parsley.

SESAME-COCONUT RICE LOAF

The trick to getting this dish to hold together is to cook the rice so that it is still slightly wet and sticky. Mushroom Cloud Gravy* is a must.

2 C cooked brown rice	1/2 C sesame butter
2 T oil	1/2 t turmeric
1 C chopped mushrooms	1 t marjoram
1 onion, diced	1/2 t ginger
1 C chopped celery	1/2 t coriander
1/2 C shredded coconut	1/2 t cumin
2 cloves garlic, pressed	1/2 t cinnamon
1 C grated carrot	

Mix the rice, oil, garlic, turmeric, ginger, marjoram, coriander, cumin, cinnamon and sesame butter very well in a large bowl. Fold in remaining ingredients. Oil a 9" x 5" loaf pan, pack in the rice mixture and bake at 350° for 45 minutes until well browned on top.

THE DARK CONTINENT

Lentils and millet are two of the principal foods of Africa. This combination produces a delicious loaf that can be complemented by your favorite gravy.

2 C lentils	1 t mineral salt
1 C millet, cooked	1/2 t each: thyme, basil and
1 large onion, diced	cinnamon
2 cloves garlic, pressed	1/4 t black pepper

Cook the lentils until soft, drain and mix with the millet. Add the remaining ingredients and mix well. Pack into an oiled 9" x 5" loaf pan and bake at 350° for 45 minutes.

EGGPLANT TOFUSAN

A journey to Italy — via China. Serve with rice for a splendid repast.

2 large eggplants	1 lb tofu*
Oil	2 onions, chopped
4 C tomato sauce*	Basil, oregano and sesame seeds

Cut the eggplants into ½" slices. Cook them on an oiled skillet until brown on both sides. In another skillet, sauté the onion in ½ T of oil until clear. Put a thin layer of sauce (1 C) in a 9" x 13" baking dish. Follow with a layer of eggplant slices, half the tofu (sliced) and all of the onions. Follow this with the remaining eggplant slices, tofu and sauce. Sprinkle with herbs and seeds and bake for ½ hour at 400°.

THE CREATIVE TOSTADA

Winner of the Pancho Villa Tostada Award. Need I say more?

2 C tomato sauce*	1/4 t cayenne
Juice of 2 lemons	1 t each cumin, mineral salt
1-1/2 C kidney beans	and paprika
1 onion, diced	Tortillas or chapatis*
1 tomato, diced	Shredded lettuce, chopped
2 cloves garlic, pressed	onion, and sprouts

Soak the beans in water overnight, then cook them in about 4-½ C water, with the onion and tomato, until tender. Add the seasonings and mix well. Add the tomato sauce and lemon juice and mix again. To serve, spread some beans on a tortilla or chapati; arrange lettuce and sprouts on top and sprinkle with chopped onion.

MILLET AND VEGETABLES
The dish to prepare when you're pressed for time.

1 C millet	1 T oil
1 carrot, sliced	1 T kelp
1 C sliced cabbage	Soy sauce substitute
1 C cauliflower pieces	

Cook the millet in 3 C water until almost all the water is gone. Add vegetables and cook for another 5-10 minutes. Add oil and kelp, season with soy sauce substitute and serve.

CAST A GIANT SHADOW
Created as a sacrifice to the moon during a lunar eclipse in Taurus. It worked . . .

1 C cooked rice	1 T paprika
2 C cooked garbanzo beans,	1/2 t celery seed
mashed	1/2 t white pepper
1 C cooked millet	1 t cumin
2 C cooked and mashed	1 T oregano
Jerusalem artichokes	2 t mineral salt
1 C grated carrots	1 t coriander
2 tomatoes, chopped	1/4 t cloves
2 onions, diced and sautéed in	4 cloves garlic, pressed
2 T oil	

Mix all ingredients very well in a huge bowl. Press into an oiled 9" x 13" baking dish and bake for 45 minutes at 350°. Serve with your favorite gravy.

STUFFED VEGETABLES

Almost any vegetable can be stuffed, but by far the most popular ones are eggplants, peppers, tomatoes and zucchini. Eggplants and zucchini can be stuffed by removing their tops and scooping out their insides, or by halving them and scooping them out. For peppers, simply cut off the tops of bells, or slice the long varieties lengthwise. Tomatoes should have their tops cut off and insides scooped out. In the case of the eggplants, zucchini and tomatoes, their pulp should be chopped and added to the filling, too.

Here is a basic recipe for stuffed vegetables, followed by three stuffing recipes:

6 large bell peppers or	6 medium zucchini
3 medium eggplants or	1 recipe for stuffing
6 large tomatoes or	

Prepare the vegetables as in the above explanation. Fill with stuffing. If there is stuffing left over, arrange it on the bottom of a baking dish, set vegetables on top and bake at 350° for 30-45 minutes.

RICE STUFFING

2 C cooked rice	1 C chopped celery
2 T oil	2 t thyme
1 onion, diced	1 t cinnamon
1 C chopped mushrooms	Mineral salt and white pepper

Sauté the onion, mushrooms, celery and thyme in the oil for 5 minutes. Add remaining ingredients, and mix well.

SAHARA STUFFING

2 C cooked lentils

1 onion, diced

2 T chopped parsley

1/2 t mineral salt

1 t cumin

1/4 t black pepper

2 carrots, grated

Combine all ingredients, mixing well.

COCONUT-MILLET STUFFING

2 C cooked millet

1 C fresh coconut, cut in thin slices

1/2 C grated beets

1 carrot grated

1/2 t nutmeg

1/2 t mineral salt

Combine ingredients, mixing well.

RAT-A-TAT WILLY IN A WOK
A spicy dish from Algeria.   They call it Ratatouille.

1 onion, chopped

1/4 C oil

1-1/2 t basil

1-1/2 t oregano

2 cloves garlic, pressed

1 lb zucchini, sliced thickly

1 eggplant, cut in cubes

2 bell peppers, sliced

4 tomatoes, cut in wedges

1 C tomato sauce*

1/4 t cayenne

Heat the oil in the wok, add the onion, basil, oregano and garlic, and stir fry until the onion turns clear. Add the zucchini and eggplant, and stir fry for 5 minutes. Add the remaining ingredients, stir, cover and cook for 30-45 minutes on LOW heat.

JUST KIBBING

A variation of Kibbeh, the national dish of Syria and Lebanon.

1 lb cauliflower	1 eggplant, cut in 1" cubes
1 large onion, grated	1/2 C sunflower seeds or
3 C cooked millet	pine nuts
1/2 t black pepper	1 t mineral salt
1 onion, chopped	1/2 t white pepper
3 T oil	1 t cinnamon

Steam and mash the cauliflower. Mix with the grated onion, millet and black pepper. Set aside. Sauté the chopped onion in the oil until clear. Add eggplant and sunflower seeds or pine nuts, and cook until eggplant is soft. Add remaining ingredients, and mix well. Set aside. Oil a 9" x 13" baking dish. Spread half the cauliflower mixture on the bottom. Follow this with the eggplant mixture and top with the remaining cauliflower mixture. Drizzle an additional 2 T oil over the top and bake at 375° for 30-45 minutes until brown on top.

META-FALAFEL

An Egyptian recipe that's as old as the Pharaohs.

1 lb garbanzo beans	2 t each: cumin, coriander and
2 red onions, grated	mineral salt
3 cloves garlic, pressed	1/4 t cayenne
1/2 bunch finely chopped parsley	Oil to fry

Soak the garbanzos in water overnight. Drain. Grind the beans in a flour mill or meat grinder. Add the remaining ingredients and mix very well. Adjust seasoning if necessary.

There are 2 ways to cook the falafels. The traditional way is to roll the mixture into 1" balls and deep fry until well browned. An alternative is to form the mix into patties about ½" thick and 2" round. Fry each side on an oiled skillet until brown. Serve with Sesame Sauce*.

MOROCCAN TAGINE
A vegetable stew from the back alleys of Marrakech.

1 lb potatoes, sliced	1/2 t each: mineral salt, cumin,
1 cauliflower, cut in pieces	and oregano
1 broccoli, cut in pieces	1/4 t each: dill, marjoram, bay
1 lb carrots, sliced	leaf, thyme, black pepper
2 onions, halved and sliced	Pinch of each: white pepper,
2 C peas	cayenne, turmeric, nutmeg,
2 T olive oil	cinnamon, allspice, cloves,
3 cloves garlic, pressed	ginger, coriander and
1 T paprika	cardamon

Layer the vegetables in a very large pot in the following manner: potatoes, carrots, cauliflower, broccoli, onions and peas. In a small bowl, mix the olive oil, garlic and all of the herbs and spices. Add 2 C water, mix well and pour over the vegetables. Bring to a boil, cover and steam on lowest possible heat for 1-½ to 2 hours until vegetables are well cooked. Check frequently, adding water as needed. Mix vegetables before serving.

BREADS, MUFFINS AND BISCUITS

SQUARE BREAD

The rice flour gives this bread its heavier texture and somewhat dense appearance.

3/4 C soy flour	2 T nutritional yeast (optional)
1 C rice flour	2 T honey
1/4 C corn meal	3 T oil
1 t baking powder	1 C water
1 t mineral salt	

Mix honey, oil and water. Mix remaining ingredients and add to liquid, stirring well. Pour into oiled 8" x 8" x 2" pan and bake for 35-40 minutes at 300° until well browned, and toothpick inserted in center of bread comes out clean.

FOUR FLOUR LOAF

Crispy outside, soft and delicate inside. Holds up to a sandwich.

2 C soy flour	3 t baking powder
1 C corn meal	1/4 C oil
1/2 C rice flour	1/3 C honey
1/2 C lima bean flour	2-1/4 C water
1 t mineral salt	

Mix flours, salt and baking powder in a large bowl. Add honey, water and oil mixing well. Add more water, if necessary, until a cake batter consistency is reached. Pour batter into oiled 9" x 5" loaf pan and bake for 1-½ hours at 275° until well browned and toothpick inserted in center of loaf comes out clean.

WARREN'S QUASI-STELLAR CORN BREAD
My personal favorite and the easiest to prepare. I only wish I could take credit for its development.

1 C soy flour	2 t baking powder
1 C corn meal	1-2/3 C warm water
Pinch mineral salt	2 T honey

Mix water and honey. Mix dry ingredients. Heavily oil a 10" cast iron skillet and place in oven for 5 minutes. Add liquid to dry ingredients, stirring only until just mixed. Pour into hot skillet and bake at 400° for 15-20 minutes until brown around edge.

This recipe can easily be made into muffins by increasing the baking powder to 4 t and then following the rest of the recipe as is. Fill oiled muffin tins 2/3 full, and bake at 375° for 15-20 minutes.

ZARITA'S CRANBERRY CORN BREAD
Cindy stopped moving long enough to create this most delicious sweetbread. Add nuts for variety.

2-1/2 C corn meal	Juice of 1 orange
1 C soy flour	Grated peel of 1 orange
3/4 C honey	1 t vanilla
1/2 C oil	1 C raisins
1 C water	1 C cranberries, chopped

Mix flours together. Add honey, water and oil, and mix very well. Add vanilla, orange peel and juice, raisins and cranberries. Mix again. Pour into an oiled 9" x 5" loaf pan and bake at 325° for 40-50 minutes, testing with toothpick. Cool before removing from pan.

COLORFUL CARROT BREAD

It's the corn meal that really makes this one. . .or maybe it's the carrots. . .the nutmeg. . .?

1 C soy flour	1 t cinnamon
1 C corn meal	1/4 t nutmeg
1/2 t mineral salt	1-3/4 C water
1 C grated carrot	1/4 C honey
2 t baking powder	

Mix honey and water and add to remaining ingredients mixing well. Pour mixture into heavily oiled 10" cast iron skillet, 9" round cake pan, or 8" x 8" x 2" pan. Bake for 20 minutes at 375°, testing with toothpick.

CHAPATIS

Chapatis are the flat, pan-baked breads of India. Any combinations of flours will do. The wheatless variety is not as crisp as the original, but is still incredibly delicious—and very easy to prepare.

1/2 C soy flour	1 T honey
1/4 C corn meal	1/2 T mineral salt
1 T oil	1/2 C water

Combine all ingredients, mixing well. Set a skillet over a medium flame and oil it well. Pour in about 3 T of batter and spread it out so that it is round and 6" in diameter. When brown, turn and cook other side. Serve hot.

CORN TORTILLAS

The corn meal makes these slightly gritty, so exercise your teeth; they're worth the effort.

1 C corn meal	1 t mineral salt
3/4 C water	

Mix the corn meal and water and let stand for 30 minutes. Stir in mineral salt and cook on oiled skillet.

MEGA-MUFFINS
As the name implies, these are positively atomic. Delicious with fresh pear butter.

1-1/2 C soy flour	4 t baking powder
3/4 C lima bean flour	1/3 C oil
3/4 C corn meal	1/4 C honey
1 t mineral salt	

Combine ingredients, mixing well. Fill oiled muffin tins 2/3 full. Bake at 375° for 15-20 minutes until brown.

WEIGHTLESS BISCUITS
Also called space biscuits! Light, airy little puffs ready to be dunked in gravy or smothered in jam.

1/2 C soy flour	2 t honey
1/2 C lima bean flour	2 T oil
1/2 t mineral salt	1/3 C water
2 t baking powder	

Combine ingredients, mixing well. Drop by spoonfuls onto oiled baking sheet. Bake for 12-15 minutes at 325° until brown on edges.

YEASTED BISCUITS

Heavier than the preceding recipe, but an interesting change of pace.

1 T dry active yeast	1/4 C warm water
1 t honey	

———————————————————

1/2 C corn meal	2 T oil
1/2 C soy flour	2 T honey
1 C rice flour	1/4 t mineral salt
2 T oil	3-4 T warm water

Dissolve the yeast in the water and add 1 t honey. Leave in a warm place for 10 minutes. Add the remaining ingredients, mixing well. Cover and let rise for 1 hour. Knead briefly, form into flat cakes about 2" round and place on an oiled baking sheet. Bake at 300° for 15-20 minutes.

CAKES, FROSTINGS AND COOKIES

BLUEBERRY COBBLER

Serve this one warm on a cool summer's night in the mountains when everyone gets hungry all of a sudden. . . for some strange reason.

1 lb blueberries	1/4 C corn meal
1 T arrowroot	1/3 C soy flour
1/2 t nutmeg	1/3 C rice flour
1/2 t coriander	1/3 C lima bean flour
1 t grated lemon rind	1 t baking powder
3/4 C honey	1/2 t mineral salt
2 T water	1/3 C oil

Combine first set of ingredients in an 8" x 8" x 2" pan, and simmer on top of stove for 2 minutes. Combine second set of ingredients and sprinkle over top of fruit mixture in pan.   Bake for 20 minutes at 300° until top is browned. NOTE: Other fruit, such as cherries or apricots can be substituted for the blueberries.

INDESCRIBABLE PINEAPPLE UPSIDE-DOWN CAKE

Also called "Not-to-be-Believed Pineapple Upside-Down Cake". Make it for your mother when she comes to visit—she won't believe it either.

1 large or medium pineapple	1 t vanilla
1 C hot water	1 C soy flour
1/4 C honey	1 C corn meal
1/2 C oil	1/2 t mineral salt

1/3 C honey   2 t baking powder

1 C water

Cut pineapple into small chunks and line bottom of oiled 8" x 8" x 2" pan. Mix honey and water and pour over fruit. Place dish in oven. Combine remaining oil, honey and water. Mix remaining ingredients and add to liquid ingredients, stirring well. Pour over fruit and bake for 45-50 minutes at 300° until brown on top. Cool in pan, then turn over onto a flat dish.

COSMIC CARROT CAKE
Guaranteed to raise anyone's consciousness. Recipe developed by Captain Midnite.

2 C grated raw carrot	1/2 t nutmeg
1 C soy flour	1 t mineral salt
1/2 C lima bean flour	2/3 C water
1/2 C corn meal	1/4 C lemon juice
1/2 C honey or maple syrup	3 t baking powder
1/2 C oil	1/2-1 C raisins (optional)
1 t cinnamon	

Combine grated carrot, flours, salt, baking powder, raisins and spices in a large bowl. Mix honey, oil, water and lemon juice and add to dry ingredients, mixing well. Pour into oiled 9" x 13" x 2" pan, and bake at 300° for 45 minutes, testing with a toothpick.

PLUM INCREDIBLE CAKE
Came back from plum picking one day and dreamed up this one. Even better than the name implies.

2 C soy flour	1/4 t cloves
2 C corn meal	3 C pitted plums
1/2 t mineral salt	2 1/2 C water
3 t baking powder	2 T rose water (optional)
1 t allspice	Honey

Simmer the plums in the water gently until soft. Add honey to taste and set aside to cool to room temperature. Combine remaining ingredients. Add plum mixture and mix well. Pour into heavily oiled 9" x 13" x 2" pan. Bake for 45 minutes at 300°, testing with toothpick. NOTE: An interesting variation is Plum Nuts Cake. Simply add 1 C chopped nuts to the batter, and bake as directed.

OLDE ENGLANDE GINGERBREAD

If Wordsworth were alive today, I'm sure he'd demand this one!

1/2 C oil	1/2 t mineral salt
1/4 C honey	2 t baking powder
1/4 C water	1 t cinnamon
1 C molasses	1 t cloves
1/2 C corn meal	1 1/2 t ginger
1/2 C lima bean flour	1 C hot water
1 1/2 C soy flour	

Beat oil, honey and ¼ C water. Add molasses and beat. Mix remaining ingredients, except hot water. Add to liquid ingredients, alternately with hot water, beating for 2-3 minutes. Pour into oiled 9" x 13" x 2" pan, and bake for 1 hour at 300° testing with toothpick.

LIGHT AND LOVELY MARBLE CAKE

Soft and spongy, this cake is great for birthdays and holidays because of its festive appearance.

1 C honey	1 1/2 C water
1 C oil	1 1/2 C soy flour
1/2 C sesame butter	1 C lima bean flour
3 t vanilla	3 t baking powder
1 t mineral salt	1/2 C carob powder

In blender mix the honey, oil and sesame butter. Add vanilla and salt and pour mixture into bowl. Add remaining ingredients, except carob powder, stirring well. Pour all but ½ C batter into oiled 9" x 13" x 2" pan, or two 9" round cake pans. Add carob powder to remaining batter, plus enough water to return consistency to that of original batter (2-4 T). Pour carob mixture over batter in pans and swirl in with a knife to marbleize. Bake 9" x 13" x 2" pan one hour, or in 9" round pans 45-50 minutes, at 275°, testing with toothpick. NOTE: For Carob Cake simply add the carob powder when adding the remaining ingredients and proceed accordingly.

KING OF BROWNIES

So moist and chewy you'll wish you had made a second batch. Perfect every time.

1 C rice flour	1 C chopped nuts
3/4 C soy flour	1/2 C honey
1/4 C lima bean flour	1/4 C oil
1/2 C carob powder	1 t vanilla
1 1/2 t baking powder	1 1/4 C water
1 t mineral salt	

Combine flours, carob powder, baking powder, salt and nuts. Mix honey, oil, vanilla and water, and add to dry ingredients, stirring well. Pour into oiled 8" x 8" x 2" pan. Bake 45 minutes for cake-like brownies, or 35 minutes for chewier, fudgier ones, at 325°.

FROSTINGS

Any of these frostings will make the perfect topping for the cake of your choice:

UNCOOKED TROPICAL FROSTING

2 ripe bananas

1 C (or more) unsweetened

   coconut

1/2 C fresh pineapple

1/4 t vanilla or 1 t orange-

   blossom water

Pinch coriander

Mash pineapple and bananas. Add remaining ingredients plus honey to taste.

CAROB FROSTING

1/3 C carob powder

1/4 C honey

1 t vanilla

1 T oil

1/4 C water

Mix all ingredients in blender, or increase the water to ½ C, and 1 T arrowroot, and heat mixture in saucepan until it thickens. Spread on cake while hot and let cool.

CLOUD NINE

2/3 C soy milk powder

1 C water

Lemon juice and honey

2 T oil

In blender, mix the soy milk powder, water, oil, and honey to taste. Add just enough lemon juice to thicken. Chill, and use as you would any other whipped topping.

E-Z VANILLA COOKIES
When the cupboard is bare and those unexpected guests arrive, you can whip these up in no time. Try adding bits of dried fruit or fresh berries.

1/2 C honey	1 C soy flour
2 t vanilla	1/4 C lima bean flour
1/2 C oil	

Beat honey, vanilla and oil. Stir in flours; batter should be thick. Drop by spoonfuls onto oiled cookie sheet. Bake 15 minutes at 300° until brown on edges.

SUNFLOWER SEED COOKIES
Soft, and melt-in-your mouth.

1/3 C honey	1 C soy flour
2/3 C oil	1/2 C lima bean flour
1/2 t vanilla	1 C sunflower seeds
1/2 C water	

Beat honey, oil, vanilla and water. Add flour, and mix well. Stir in seeds. Spoon onto lightly oiled cookie sheet, spreading out to make 3" circles. Bake for 12-15 minutes at 300° until brown on edge.

ALMOND COOKIES
This wheatless, oriental stand-by is crunchy and rich in almond flavor.

1/4 C oil	1 1/2 C soy flour
1/2 C honey	1/2 C rice flour
1/2 C water	1/2 C lima bean flour
1 t almond extract	Almonds

Beat oil, honey, water and almond extract. Mix flours together and add to liquid mixture, combining well. Roll into golf-ball-size rounds and flatten on oiled cookie sheet. Press an almond into each cookie. Bake 15-20 minutes at 300° until lightly browned.

SESAME COOKIES
Have a calcium boost when your sweet tooth starts calling.

1/2 C honey	1 C sesame seeds
1/2 C oil	1 C soy flour
1/4 C + 2 T water	1/2 C lima bean flour
1/2 t mineral salt	

Beat honey, oil, water and salt. Add seeds and flours, mixing well. Drop by spoonfuls onto oiled cookie sheet, and bake 10-12 minutes at 325° until brown on edges.

FRUIT VOLCANOS AND HOT SPRINGS
This may sound complicated but the original recipe only took me 15 minutes to make—and about 5 minutes to devour.

3/4 C lima bean flour	1/4 C water
3/4 C rice flour	1 T orange-blossom water
1 C soy flour	Fruit preserves or jam
2/3 C oil	Cinnamon
2 T honey	

Mix flours. Add oil, honey, water, and orange-blossom water, mixing well. To make the volcanos, take a ball of dough about 1-½" round, hollow it out with your thumb and shape into a cone. Fill the cone with jam or preserves and set on top of a flat, circular piece of dough on an oiled cookie sheet. Break off the top of the cone or make a few cracks in it (or leave as is). Sprinkle with cinnamon and bake at 300° for 15-20 minutes. To make Hot Springs, form each ball of dough into a tub with your fingers (pinching up the sides). Fill with jam or preserves, place on an oiled cookie sheet and bake as above.

GINGERSNAPS

The thinner the snappier. Great with hot tea when the day is done..

1/4 C oil	1/2 C lima bean flour
1/4 C honey	1/4 t mineral salt
1/2 C molasses	1 t cinnamon
1/4 C hot water	1 t cloves
1 1/2 C soy flour	2 t ginger
1/2 C rice flour	

Beat oil and honey. Add molasses and beat, then add water and continue to beat for one minute. Mix remaining ingredients and add slowly to liquid mixture, stirring constantly until well blended. Mixture will be very thick. Take golf-ball-size pieces and flatten on an oiled cookie sheet. Bake for 15-20 minutes at 300° until dark and crisp.

PIES AND ICE CREAM

PIE CRUSTS

These pie crusts are easy because you just press them into place. My favorite is the "Pie Crust Exotica", but each recipe has a flavor and texture all its own. Ginny says to try rolling them out between layers of waxed paper.

SIMPLEST PIE CRUST

1 C soy flour	1/3 C oil
1/2 C lima bean flour	1/4 t mineral salt
1/2 C corn meal	1/3 - 1/2 C water
2 T honey	

Combine flours. Combine remaining ingredients and add to flours, mixing well. Press into well oiled 10" pie plate.

PIE CRUST EXOTICA

1 C rice flour	1/4 C maple syrup
1/2 C corn meal	1 t coriander
1/2 C lima bean flour	1/4 C water
1/4 C oil	

Combine flours. Work in the oil, then add the remaining ingredients, and mix very well. Press into well oiled 10" pie plate.

NOTE: Either of these pie crusts can be baked at 300° for 20-30 min. and used whenever a prebaked crust is needed.

MOM'S APPLE PIE

Mom's was great, but this one's better. I wish Mom had made it like this when I was a kid.

1 unbaked 10" pie crust

4 C sliced, cored apples

1 T lemon juice

1/2 t nutmeg

1/2 C raisins

1/2 C honey

1 t cinnamon

1 T arrowroot

_____

1/4 C corn meal

1/4 C soy flour

1-1/2 T oil

1/4 C date sugar

1/4 C sunflower seeds

In a large bowl gently toss the first set of ingredients, and arrange in pie crust. Combine remaining ingredients adding just enough water to make a crumbly mixture. Sprinkle over top of pie, and bake for 45 minutes at 300°. Alternatively you can sprinkle the pie with date sugar or seeds or nuts. . . Combine them all, or leave it plain.

TROPICAL NUT PIE

Take a vacation to the South Seas without ever leaving your kitchen table. This one's sure to come back for an encore.

1 prebaked 10" pie crust

1 C pitted dates

2 C water

2 T arrowroot, 1 t coriander

1 C cashews, chopped

2 bananas

In blender, mix dates, water, arrowroot and coriander. Place mixture in saucepan and stir over heat until very thick. Add cashews. Slice bananas into baked pie shell and pour date mixture over all. Let cool, then chill in refrigerator.

BANANA CREAMLESS PIE

This one takes a little time and a few bowls, but the end result is a knockout. The riper the bananas, the better the pie.

2 T agar agar flakes

1/2 C water

1/4 C honey

2/3 C ground cashews or sesame
   seeds

6 T arrowroot

1 t vanilla

1 t cinnamon

2 C water

2 C mashed ripe bananas

1 prebaked 10" pie crust

Dissolve agar agar flakes in ½ C water and let sit one minute. Bring to a boil and simmer 1 minute. Set aside. Mix remaining ingredients, except banana, in blender until very smooth. Pour into saucepan and stir constantly over heat until very thick. Add agar mixture and mashed banana and mix well. Pour into pie shell. Cool, then chill in refrigerator.

Variations: (1) Add 1 C shredded coconut. (2) Replace mashed bananas with sliced bananas and line pie shell with these. Pour mixture over all.

COCONUT CREAMLESS PIE
The Exotica pie crust was made for this pie. Utter joy.

1 prebaked 10" pie crust

1 t cardamon

3 T arrowroot

1 1/2 T agar agar flakes

1/2 C water

3 C fresh coconut milk*

Pinch of cloves

2 T honey

2 T rosewater

1/2 C shredded coconut

Mix everything in a blender except the agar agar and water. Heat in saucepan, stirring frequently, until thick. Meanwhile soak the agar agar flakes in ¼ C hot water for 1 minute. Add another ¼ C water and boil for 1 minute. Add to coconut mixture after it's thick. Pour into pie shell, cool and chill. Top with Cloud Nine* if desired.

VANILLA ICE CREAM
Proof that you can make anything from soybeans.

1/4 C oil	1 C soy milk powder
1/2 C honey	2 1/2 C water
1 T vanilla	

Blend the ingredients well and freeze in trays. Add fruit and/or nuts for variety. NOTE: For a creamier ice cream, beat the mixture after it's been frozen and refreeze.

MAPLE NUT ICE CREAM
Vermonters will love this one.

1/2 C maple syrup	1 C soy milk powder
1 T maple extract	3 C water
1 T vanilla	1 C walnuts

Blend all the ingredients (except walnuts) well. Stir in walnuts, and freeze as above.

SWEET TREATS

These are great for holidays and all those special occasions when you want to add that something extra.

SESAME FINGERS

3 C sesame seeds	1/2 C date sugar
1 1/2 C shredded coconut	1/4 t vanilla
4 T sesame butter	1/2 C chopped nuts
1/2 C honey	

Preheat oven to 300°. Mix all ingredients very well and press into oiled cookie sheet ½" thick. Bake 20-30 minutes. Cool thoroughly and cut into 3" fingers.

CAROB FUDGE

1/2 C oil, 1/2 C honey	1/2 C chopped nuts
1/2 t vanilla	1 C carob powder

Beat oil, honey and vanilla until very smooth. Stir in nuts and carob powder. Press into lightly oiled 8" x 8" x 2" pan and chill to harden.

SCENTED ALMOND BALLS

1 1/2 C ground almonds	Honey
2 T orange-blossom water	Shredded coconut

Combine orange-blossom water and ground almonds. Add enough honey to make a stiff mixture. Shape into balls and roll in coconut.

HALVAH

1 C sesame seeds	1 T honey

Grind seeds in blender. Work in honey and knead until the mixture has the consistency of hard dough. Serve as is or break into pieces and roll in coconut or whole seeds. Raisins, nuts or grated carrot may also be added before working in the honey.

FRUIT CHEWS

1 C pitted dates	1 C walnuts
1 C dried apricots	1 C coconut
1 C raisins	3 T lemon juice

Grind the fruit and nuts, stir in the lemon juice, roll in shredded coconut or seeds and chill.

GOOD CANDY

1 lb dried apricots	1/4 t grated fresh ginger
1 t cinnamon	3 t freshly ground cardamon
1 T sesame butter	seed
Honey	Shredded coconut

Soak the apricots in water to cover overnight. Chop the apricots, add honey to taste, sesame butter and spices. Work in enough coconut to hold the mixture together. Roll into balls and chill.